Exploring the New World

An Interactive History Adventure

by Melody Herr

Consultant:
John P. Boubel, PhD
History Professor, Bethany Lutheran College
Mankato, Minnesota

Capstone
press

Mankato, Minnesota

You Choose Books are published by Capstone Press,
151 Good Counsel Drive, P.O. Box 669, Mankato, Minnesota 56002.
www.capstonepress.com

Library of Congress Cataloging-in-Publication Data
Herr, Melody.
   Exploring the new world: an interactive history adventure / by Melody Herr.
   p. cm. — (You choose books)
   Summary: "Describes the exploration of North America in the times of explorers
Christopher Columbus, Francisco Vázquez de Coronado, and Sieur de La Salle. The
reader's choices reveal the historical details from Columbus' voyage in 1492, Coronado's
1540 expedition, and Sieur de La Salle's expedition down the Mississippi River in 1682" —
Provided by publisher.
   Includes bibliographical references and index.
   ISBN-13: 978-1-4296-1357-6 (hardcover)   ISBN-13: 978-1-4296-1764-2 (softcover)
   ISBN-10: 1-4296-1357-2 (hardcover)   ISBN-10: 1-4296-1764-0 (softcover)
   1. America — Discovery and exploration — Juvenile literature. 2. Columbus,
Christopher — Juvenile literature. 3. Coronado, Francisco Vásquez de, 1510–1554 —
Juvenile literature. 4. La Salle, Robert Cavelier, sieur de, 1643–1687 — Juvenile literature. I.
Title. II. Series.
E101.H47 2008
970.01 — dc22   2007034971

Editorial Credits

Rebecca Glaser and Christopher L. Harbo, editors; Juliette Peters, set designer;
   Gene Bentdahl, book designer; Danielle Ceminsky, illustrator; Wanda Winch,
   photo researcher

Photo credits

Art Resource, N.Y./ Smithsonian American Art Museum, Washington, DC, 53; Art Resource, N.Y./Erich Lessing, 10; Art Resource, N.Y./
Scala, 60; Art Resource, N.Y./Snark, 45; Art Resource, N.Y./The Newark Museum, 31; Corbis/Blue Lantern Studio, 80; Courtesy of the
artist, Charles Banks Wilson, 85; Courtesy Palace of the Governors (MNM/DCA), Kenneth Chapman, #048918, 57; Courtesy, Arkansas
History Commission, 79; Dorling Kindersley/Peter Dennis, 34; Kansas State Historical Society, 48; Library of Congress, 13; Mary Evans
Picture Library, 43, 100; North Wind Picture Archives, 16, 26, 39, 65; Ohio Historical Society, 95; Photri-MicroStock/John Morrell &
Co. Ottumwa, Iowa Collection/B. Howe/N.C. Wyeth Painting, 40; The Art Archive/Musee des Arts Africains et Oceaniens/Gianni Dagli
Orti, 72; The Bridgeman Art Library/©Brooklyn Museum of Art, New York, USA/ Dick S. Ramsay Fund and Healy Purchase Fund B/
Columbus before the Queen, 1843 (oil on canvas) by Emanuel Gottlieb Leutze (1816-68), 28; The Bridgeman Art Library/©Museu de
Marinha, Lisbon, Portugal/Portrait of John II of Portugal (1455-95) (panel) by Portuguese School (15th century), 24; The Bridgeman
Art Library/©Private Collection/ Peter Newark American Pictures/Zuni Tribesman, 1854 (colour litho) by American School (19th
century), 63; The Bridgeman Art Library/Index/ ©Museo Naval, Madrid, Spain/Portrait of Martin Alonzo Pinzon (d.1493) by Spanish
School (16th century), 19; The Mariners' Museum, Newport News. Virginia, 6, 71; The New York Public Library, Astor, Lenox and Tilden
Foundations/Picture Collection, the Branch Libraries., 88; The New York Public Library, Astor, Lenox and Tilden Foundations/Print
Collection, Miriam and Ira D. Wallach Division of Art, Prints and Photographs, cover; William K. Hartmann, 67

1 2 3 4 5 6 13 12 11 10 09 08

TABLE OF CONTENTS

ABOUT YOUR ADVENTURE

YOU live in an era of exploration. Will you explore the New World with European adventurers — or will you protect it with the American Indians who have always called it home? How will your choices impact your life?

In this book, you'll explore how the choices people made meant the difference between life and death. The events you'll experience happened to real people.

Chapter One sets the scene. Then you choose which path to read. Follow the directions at the bottom of each page. The choices you make will change your outcome. After you finish one path, go back and read the others for new perspectives and more adventures.

*YOU CHOOSE the path
you take through history.*

Early European explorers traveled several months across the Atlantic Ocean to reach the New World.

Discoveries

It is a time of great discoveries. For Europeans, North America and South America are the New World. Explorers set out to claim land, spread their religion, and find riches.

Due to these European visitors, life for the native people changes forever. Explorers bring new words and a new religion to the American Indians. They bring unfamiliar tools, plants, and animals. They also bring terrible diseases.

Turn the page.

Your adventure into the New World will introduce you to Christopher Columbus, Francisco Vázquez de Coronado, and René-Robert Cavelier, Sieur de La Salle. Each one explores a different part of the New World in a different century. Each meets a different group of native people.

Columbus sails from Spain in 1492. Spices, silk, and jewels from Asia bring high prices in Europe. But traveling eastward across Europe to Asia takes many months and is very expensive. Columbus believes he can find a cheaper shortcut by sailing west across the Atlantic Ocean. But Columbus doesn't know that North and South America lie in the way.

In 1540, stories about the Seven Cities of Cíbola spread through Spain's American colonies. Coronado hopes to find fame and riches by searching for these cities made of gold. But he doesn't have a map.

In December 1681, La Salle sets out from Lake Michigan. He plans to canoe down the Mississippi River to the Gulf of Mexico to claim land for the king of France. He's ready to face wild animals, unfriendly Indians, and other unknown dangers.

→ To meet Columbus, turn to page **11**.

→ To meet Coronado, turn to page **41**.

→ To meet La Salle, turn to page **73**.

Christopher Columbus led three ships, the *Niña*, the *Pinta*, and the *Santa Maria*, across the Atlantic Ocean in 1492.

CHAPTER 2

Christopher Columbus

Today is October 12, 1492. Three ships sail toward a string of islands. Columbus and his sailors think they've reached "the Indies," their name for East Asia. In fact, they're close to North America.

The American Indians living on these islands call themselves the "Tainos." They have never seen ships or met Europeans.

Both groups of people are about to meet. Neither group knows it, but their lives will change forever.

➤ To be a sailor on the Santa Maria, turn to page **12**.

➤ To be a Tainos islander, turn to page **30**.

At midnight, you stand on the deck of the *Santa Maria*. You squint, trying to see into the night. The other two ships, the *Niña* and the *Pinta*, look like shadows. You really hope to see land soon.

When Columbus told you King Ferdinand and Queen Isabella of Spain sponsored his voyage, you joined eagerly. Now, though, you've been sailing for more than two months. Columbus' "shortcut" to the Indies doesn't seem so short. You can't wait to tour the cities and buy spices, silk, and jewels.

Boom! Boom! You hear the *Pinta*'s cannon roar. That signal means the crew sees land.

As the sun rises, you see an island. You row a small boat to shore with Columbus and the other two ship captains. You stick a flag and a cross in the sand to claim the island for Spain.

The people of the island gather around you on the beach. To your surprise, these Indians aren't wearing silk robes as you would expect Asians to wear. In fact, they're not wearing anything but loincloths!

Columbus' men planted a flag in the sand to claim the island for Spain.

Turn the page.

"Where's the city of your ruler, the Great Khan?" you ask. Since the Indians don't speak Spanish, you try using sign language. They point across the water.

Columbus leads the fleet from island to island. Instead of cities, he finds villages. After a few weeks, the captain of the *Pinta*, Martín Alonso Pinzón, approaches you. "Columbus will never find the Great Khan's palaces. Let's take my ship and go exploring on our own."

"You mean desert Columbus? We'll go to jail," you warn.

"Not if we find the Khan's cities first. If we beat Columbus back to Spain, the queen will give us the reward," Pinzón replies.

→ To stay with Columbus, go to page **15**.

→ To join Pinzón, turn to page **18**.

You and Columbus explore an island he names Hispaniola. By now it's December. It's winter in Spain. Here on the islands, though, the days feel like spring. "The birds shine more beautifully than jewels," you think, "and the flowers smell sweeter than spices. But I still want to find the Khan's kingdom."

On Christmas Eve, the sailor in charge of the ship's tiller leaves his post. With no one to steer the *Santa Maria*, it hits a sandbar. The tide runs out, leaving the ship stranded on dry ground. With a loud crack, the ship's hull splits open.

"How will we get back to Spain?" Columbus worries. "The tiny *Niña* can't carry all the sailors."

"We should leave some men to start a colony on Hispaniola," you suggest.

Turn the page.

Columbus smiles. "Good idea. I'll name the new colony La Navidad because today is Christmas Eve." He gives orders to build a fort.

The *Santa Maria* broke apart after hitting a sandbar near the island of Hispaniola.

➤ To sail for home, go to page **17**.

➤ To stay in La Navidad, turn to page **25**.

On January 6, 1493, you climb aboard the *Niña* for the voyage back to Spain. As you sail away from Hispaniola, you spot the *Pinta*.

"There's Pinzón," you say to Columbus. "Let's arrest him!"

"No," Columbus replies, "not yet. We need his help. If the *Niña* and the *Pinta* sail together, we have a better chance of reaching home safely." Columbus sends a message to Pinzón, who comes to the *Niña* for a meeting.

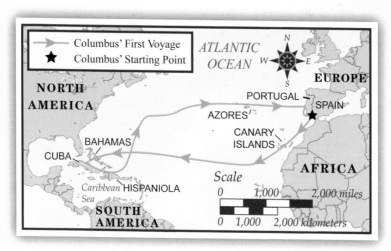

Turn to page **20.**

Pinzón sails to a large island. The Indians live in huts, but they wear gold jewelry. To your surprise, they eagerly trade their gold for broken pottery. Either gold isn't worth much to the Indians, or they're willing to pay high prices for anything from Spain.

"Where do you get this gold?" you ask. None of the Indians speak Spanish, but one woman seems to understand you. She leads you to a stream and grabs a fistful of mud. Opening her hand, she shows you shiny nuggets.

"Gold," you whisper. You trade glass beads for the nuggets. Then you race to the *Pinta*.

When you report your discovery, the sailors want to mine the gold immediately. Pinzón, however, decides to return to Spain. "We'll come back with more ships to carry all the gold," he promises the crew.

On January 6, 1493, you spot the *Niña*. As it gets closer, you see Columbus standing on the deck. "Columbus will arrest us," you warn Pinzón. "Let's get out of here!"

"No," Pinzón replies. "Crossing the ocean alone is risky. If the *Pinta* sails with Columbus' ship, we have a better chance of reaching home safely." Reluctantly, you and Pinzón go to the *Niña* for a meeting with Columbus.

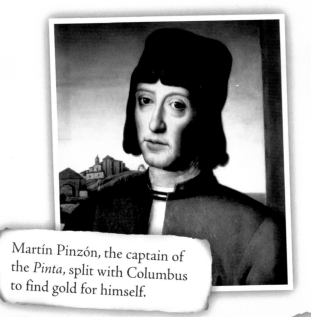

Martín Pinzón, the captain of the *Pinta*, split with Columbus to find gold for himself.

Turn the page.

"Did you find the Great Khan?" Columbus asks Pinzón.

"No, but I traded with the Indians for gold. I even found out where they get it. There are gold mines on these islands," Pinzón reports.

"I have bad news," Columbus replies. "The *Santa Maria* was wrecked, and I had to leave a group of sailors on Hispaniola. Will you sail with me to Spain?"

Pinzón agrees. You can see, though, that he doesn't trust Columbus. Columbus doesn't trust him either. "Which one do I trust?" you ask yourself.

➤ *To sail with Columbus, go to page* **21**.

➤ *To sail with Pinzón, turn to page* **27**.

On January 16, 1493, the crew hauls up the sails for the return voyage. "We'll be home soon," Columbus promises, "as long as the good weather holds."

Just then, the sky gets dark. The wind whips the sails. Waves pound the ship. Sailors begin to pray. In case he drowns, Columbus writes a letter about his discoveries, seals it in a barrel, and throws it overboard.

Thankfully, the *Niña* survives the storm. But the *Pinta* has disappeared.

"Pinzón's ship probably sank," Columbus says. "We must repair the *Niña*, or it will sink as well."

"But the nearest land is Portugal," a sailor protests. "And the Portuguese are longtime enemies of Spain."

Turn the page.

"We have no choice," Columbus replies. "Besides, I've met King João II. I'm sure he'll help us."

When the *Niña* sails into a Portuguese port on March 4, 1493, Columbus writes the king a letter. The king not only grants permission to repair the ship, but he also invites Columbus to visit. "Do you want to visit the king with me?" Columbus asks.

You pause. Years ago, Columbus asked King João II to fund a voyage, and the king refused. What will he do now when he learns Columbus found a shortcut to the Indies?

➤ *To visit the king with Columbus, go to page* **23**.

➤ *To stay with the ship's crew, turn to page* **28**.

When you get to the king's palace, the palace page announces Columbus' arrival. You and Columbus bow to the king.

"I hear you sailed to the Indies," King João says. "Tell me about your voyage." He listens while Columbus describes the strange trees, the colorful birds, and the native people he found on the islands.

"Exactly where are these islands?" the king asks as he points at Columbus' map. "A treaty signed in 1479 draws a line on the map. Spain owns the land north of the line. Portugal owns all the land south of it. I believe the islands you discovered are on my side of the line."

Turn the page.

King João II of Portugal believed he owned the islands Columbus had discovered.

"I know nothing about this treaty," Columbus replies. "I had orders to stay out of Portuguese territory — and I did." You try to look innocent, but you know the islands are on the south side of the treaty line.

"The Pope will decide who owns these new islands," King João declares. "For now, I wish you a safe journey to Spain."

You and Columbus hurry back to the *Niña*.

Turn to page **28**.

The *Niña* sails away, leaving you at the fort with 39 other sailors. Diego de Arana, Pedro Gutiérrez, and Rodrigo de Escobedo take command of the fort.

Guacanagarí, the chief of the nearby Indian village, helps you settle into your new home. Some of the Spanish sailors, however, steal from the Indians and fight among themselves. During an argument, Gutiérrez and Escobedo kill one of the sailors. They flee to another part of the island near the village of Chief Caonabó. Nine men go with them.

Arana sends you to look for the murderers. A few days later, you find Gutiérrez, wounded and lying under a tree.

"What happened?" you ask. "Where are the other men?"

Turn the page.

Indian warriors attacked La Navidad and destroyed the Spanish fort.

"Killed," Gutiérrez gasps. "Chief Caonabó's warriors attacked us because we robbed their village. Now they're heading for La Navidad."

You race back to La Navidad. Caonabó's warriors beat you there. They set fire to the fort. As you run toward the forest to hide, a spear pierces your chest. You crumple to the ground. As you struggle to breathe, you realize you will never see Spain again.

THE END

To follow another path, turn to page 9.
To read the conclusion, turn to page 101.

On January 16, 1493, the voyage to Spain begins. With a strong wind in their sails, the ships rush over the ocean.

One afternoon, clouds suddenly darken the sky. The wind roars. Waves beat the ship. Sailors are terrified. When the sea becomes calm again, you can't see the *Niña*.

"I hope Columbus and his crew drown," Pinzón says. "Then the queen will reward us for discovering the shortcut to the Indies."

When you reach Spain on March 15, 1493, you hear that the *Niña* arrived a few hours earlier. Columbus — not Pinzón — will receive the royal reward. "If only I'd stayed with Columbus," you think, "I'd be famous."

THE END

To follow another path, turn to page 9.
To read the conclusion, turn to page 101.

Columbus reported his discoveries to King Ferdinand and Queen Isabella when he returned to Spain in 1493.

"King João II gave us supplies for our voyage," Columbus tells the crew when he returns from the meeting. "Now let's go home."

On March 15, 1493, the *Niña* anchors in Palos, Spain. A few hours later, you spot familiar sails. "Look! There's the *Pinta*," you call to Columbus. "Pinzón has returned."

While the sailors celebrate their safe return, Columbus writes to King Ferdinand and Queen Isabella. As soon as they receive his letter, they invite him to meet with them. "You must come too," Columbus says, showing you the invitation.

At the royal court, Columbus announces his discovery of a new route to the Indies. As proof, he displays plants and animal skins from the islands. When he gives the queen jewelry made by the Indians, she rises from her throne.

"Admiral Columbus, you will be greatly rewarded," Queen Isabella promises. "But first you must make another voyage to these islands. I'll provide 17 ships and 1,000 men. Soon, Spain will rule the Indies."

"Thank you, Your Majesty," Columbus answers. Then he turns to you. "Will you sail with me again?"

"Of course," you reply. "When do we leave?"

THE END

To follow another path, turn to page 9.
To read the conclusion, turn to page 101.

You live on Guanahaní, an island in the Caribbean, where the weather is always warm. Your people call themselves Tainos, meaning "good" or "noble." Except for a loincloth, you don't wear clothes.

Yesterday, while your sister planted pineapples, your brother weeded the sweet potatoes. You tended the fields of corn, squash, beans, peppers, and peanuts. This morning, you plan to go fishing with your friends.

You roll out of your hammock and walk to the beach. What's that out on the water? Three boats that are much larger than your canoes float offshore. Each boat has a wood pole as large as a tree trunk in its center. Wide cloths hang from these poles. Racing home, you wake the villagers.

Tainos watched as Columbus and his crew claimed the island for Spain.

When you return to the beach with your friends, strange men are kneeling in the sand. The leader gives a speech in a language you've never heard before. Meanwhile, the men plant a flag and a cross.

The leader points to himself and says "Christopher Columbus." He swings his arm toward the ocean and says "Spain." The words sound strange, but you guess he's trying to tell you his name and the name of his home.

Turn the page.

Soon Columbus and his men start exploring Guanahaní. "What are the strangers looking for?" you ask your sister.

"Who knows?" she shrugs. "But look! A sailor gave me all these glass beads for one little piece of gold."

The following evening, Columbus waves to you and your friends. He points to his ship, then to you, then to his ship again.

"He's inviting us for a visit," you say.

"Don't go! I don't trust Columbus," your brother warns.

➻ To stay on the island, go to page **33**.

➻ To accept Columbus' invitation, turn to page **34**.

Seven of your friends go with Columbus to his ship. You wait on shore until dark, but they don't return. In the morning, Columbus' fleet sails away. "See? I was right," your brother exclaims. "Columbus kidnapped our friends."

Over the next four months, you hear news from other islanders about the Spanish. They sail around the nearby islands, asking where to find a king named "the Great Khan." But no such king lives here. The Spanish finally leave in January 1493.

In the fall, Columbus returns. This time, he has 17 ships and 1,000 men. You hope he brought your friends home. Yet, you don't know what Columbus wants, and you're afraid he has evil plans.

➤ To look for your friends, turn to page 35.

➤ To run away, turn to page 36.

With six friends, you go with Columbus to his ship. Suddenly, the sailors tie your ankles together and carry you below deck. In the morning, the ship sails away from Guanahaní.

When a sailor brings food, you point to your chest and say your name. He points to himself and says "Juan." Later, Juan unties you and lets you walk on the ship's deck.

Tainos were forced into slavery by the Spanish explorers.

34

➤ To escape, turn to page **37**.

➤ To stay onboard, turn to page **38**.

Bravely, you walk to the beach to meet the Spanish. "I want to talk to Columbus," you say to the sailors. "Take me to him."

The sailors smile and nod. They help you get into their small boat and row you to the ship. "Maybe the Spanish are trustworthy," you think, relaxing a little.

The moment you climb aboard the ship, however, two men chain your ankles together. The ship takes you to a different island where Columbus is building a new colony. He needs more workers. His men capture Tainos men and women as slaves. For the rest of your life, you work in the goldfields for your Spanish masters.

THE END

To follow another path, turn to page 9.
To read the conclusion, turn to page 101.

You run away and build a hut deep in the forest. "I'll live in this hideout until the Spanish leave," you decide. What you don't know is that the Spanish plan to stay.

Over the next few years, more and more Spanish colonists come to the islands. By the 1520s, the Tainos villages and fields are gone. Many of your people are slaves in the Spanish goldfields. The rest are dead from strange diseases. Only you, alone in the forest, keep the Tainos traditions alive.

THE END

To follow another path, turn to page 9.
To read the conclusion, turn to page 101.

When Juan isn't watching, you jump overboard. You swim to the nearest island and run into the forest.

That night, you come down with a high fever. "I must have caught a disease from the Spanish," you think. "I must get back to my village." In the morning, you're too sick to move. For three days, you sweat and shiver. On the fourth day, you die alone in the forest.

THE END

To follow another path, turn to page 9.
To read the conclusion, turn to page 101.

Over the next few weeks, Juan teaches you enough Spanish to guide Columbus around the nearby islands.

"We're going back to Spain," Juan tells you in January 1493. "Columbus wants to introduce you to the king and queen."

The stormy voyage across the Atlantic Ocean takes two months. When you land in Spain, Columbus presents you to King Ferdinand and Queen Isabella. You are proof that he discovered a new route to the Indies — the name he gives your islands.

"You will be greatly rewarded, Admiral Columbus," Queen Isabella promises. "But first you must return to the Indies and explore these islands further."

Columbus presented a few Tainos Indians to King Ferdinand and Queen Isabella when he returned to Spain in 1493.

"Thank you, Your Majesty," Columbus replies. Later, as you and Columbus leave the royal court, he turns to you. "I'll need a guide for my next voyage. You will sail with me."

"Yes, sir," you reply. You know sailing with Columbus is your only chance of getting home.

THE END

To follow another path, turn to page 9.
To read the conclusion, turn to page 101.

In 1540, conquistador Francisco Vázquez de Coronado led an army in search of cities made of gold.

CHAPTER 3

Francisco Vázquez de Coronado

Spanish adventurers called conquistadors are exploring the New World. In Mexico City, Francisco Vázquez de Coronado has heard rumors about the Seven Cities of Cíbola to the north. He is gathering an army to conquer these cities of gold and claim the land for Spain.

The Zuñi Indians, however, believe they own this land. They view the Spanish as invaders. Soon the Spanish and the Zuñi will meet face to face.

→ To be a Spanish adventurer, turn to page **42**.

→ To be a Zuñi Indian, turn to page **61**.

It's a fall day in 1539. You and Coronado are meeting with Viceroy Antonia de Mendoza in Mexico City. You are making plans for the expedition.

"Viceroy," you ask the royal official, "could these rumors about the Seven Cities of Cíbola be true?"

"If they are, the king of Spain will reward the man who finds these cities," Mendoza replies. "Coronado, when can you launch the expedition?"

"I need a few months to make plans." Coronado unrolls a map of New Spain. "There's a string of Spanish towns along this Indian trail, but our mapmakers haven't traveled beyond the frontier. We'll need guides and extra supplies for our expedition."

"I'll send ships loaded with extra supplies along the west coast," Mendoza offers.

"Excellent." Coronado nods and turns to you. "Now, my friend, you must decide whether to sail or to march with the army."

In the 1500s, Mexico City was the capital of the Spanish colonies in North America.

➤ To sail, turn to page **44**.

➤ To ride with Coronado, turn to page **47**.

On May 9, 1540, you climb aboard the ship *San Pedro* in the harbor at Acapulco. Coronado set out to find Cíbola in February. Now you are sailing with Captain Hernando de Alarcón with three ships full of supplies for the army.

The fleet sails north through the Gulf of California. In late August, the fleet reaches the northern point of the gulf, where the Buena Guía River flows into it. "I don't see Coronado's army," a sailor calls from the lookout.

"Maybe the trail took Coronado farther from the ocean than he expected. If we take boats up the river, we're sure to find him," you tell Alarcón.

"Perhaps," Alarcón replies. "But let's ask the Indians living along the river what they know about Cíbola."

When you ask the Indians along the river about Cíbola, one chief says he's heard of the place. Another says he's been there. Neither one seems to know anything about Coronado.

Captain Hernando de Alarcón led a fleet up the Gulf of California with supplies for Coronado's army.

Turn the page.

In early September, an Indian arrives at the river with news. He reports that bearded men attacked Cíbola.

"Those men must be Coronado's soldiers," Alarcón exclaims. "Let's go meet them."

But you and Alarcón are the only ones from the fleet willing to march to Cíbola. The Spanish sailors refuse to leave the ships, and the Indians refuse to guide you to Cíbola.

You and Alarcón travel many miles up the river, but you see no sign of Coronado. "Let's turn back," you say at last. Reluctantly, Alarcón agrees. Before you leave, you write letters to Coronado and bury them near a tree. So that he will find them, you carve a sign: "Alarcón came this far. There are letters at the foot of this tree." Then you float down the river, board the ships, and sail home.

Turn to page 58.

Hundreds of volunteers gather at the town of Compostela on February 22, 1540. Coronado calls for order, and the army spreads out like a parade. The army includes 62 men on foot and 230 men on horseback. Missionaries, servants, and Indian men and women also travel with the group. More than 1,500 horses and mules carry clothes, equipment, and food. Shepherds drive herds of cattle and flocks of sheep.

You follow the Indian trail north until you reach the last Spanish settlement on the frontier. "The country ahead is very rugged," the townspeople warn. Yet Coronado boldly marches onward.

Turn the page.

Coronado's army marched hundreds of miles on horseback and on foot in search of the Seven Cities of Cíbola.

For days, you trudge through rocky land. When the army arrives at the Sonora River, the scouts send bad news. Instead of golden cities, they've found Indian villages.

48

"The main army must camp near the river," Coronado decides. "I will take a few soldiers to search for Cíbola."

➻ To stay with the army, go to page **49**.

➻ To ride with Coronado, turn to page **55**.

When the army's supplies run low, you ride west to look for the viceroy's ships. But you can't find either the ships or the ocean. You return to the army's camp empty-handed.

In September 1540, a messenger brings orders from Coronado to bring the army to Cíbola. The messenger leads the army on another long march. For weeks, you climb mountains, wade rivers, and cross deserts. At last, the army stumbles into a deserted Zuñi Indian village.

"Welcome to Cíbola," the messenger announces with a sweeping gesture of his arm.

"This is a pueblo — just an adobe building," you complain. "Look at the broken walls and the black streaks left by fire."

Turn the page.

"True," the messenger admits. "There was a battle when Coronado conquered this pueblo. Then he captured the pueblos in the Tiguex region, where he's making his winter base. The army will camp there."

Nearly a year has passed since the beginning of the expedition. The supplies are gone, and everyone is cold and hungry. After you settle in Tiguex, you decide to talk to Coronado. He has just returned from a nearby pueblo with Indian prisoners.

"What started this war?" you ask.

"The Indians refused to give us food and blankets," Coronado replies. "I must prove that the Spanish rule this land."

"The Indians share as much as they can," you protest.

Coronado ignores you. Greed has changed him. Although he found no gold in Cíbola, he still dreams of riches. "I met an Indian slave called 'The Turk' who promises to guide me to the kingdom of Quivira. Will you come along?"

→ To join the search for Quivira, turn to page 52.

→ To stay in Tiguex, turn to page 54.

In April 1541, more than a year since the expedition started, you set out with Coronado and a handful of his best soldiers. The Turk leads your band north and east. You ride through rivers and canyons. Then the land becomes a smooth plain.

When you reach Quivira in the middle of the summer, you find Wichita Indians living in grass huts and wearing animal skins. They plant corn and hunt buffalo. "Where's the golden kingdom?" you ask.

"The Turk tricked us," the soldiers say. "The Indians of Tiguex wanted revenge because we destroyed their pueblos. They invented a fairy tale about the kingdom of Quivira and paid The Turk to lead us to this wasteland." As punishment for lying, The Turk is put to death.

"We'll spend another winter in Tiguex," Coronado announces. "In the spring, I'll decide what to do."

The Wichita Indians lived in grass huts well after Coronado's expedition.

Turn to page **59.**

You spend the summer of 1541 in Tiguex. When Coronado returns in the fall, you hurry to greet him. "What did you find in Quivira?" you ask.

"Nothing but herds of buffalo," Coronado answers angrily. "The Indians of Quivira live in grass huts. They don't have any gold."

"What about The Turk's stories about the kingdom of Quivira?" you wonder.

"Lies — all lies! The Indians of Tiguex invented a fairy tale. They hoped we'd get lost searching for Quivira and die in the wilderness." Coronado climbs off his horse. "We'll spend another winter in Tiguex. In the spring, I'll decide what to do."

Turn to page 59.

The trail leads northeast to what seems to be the loneliest land on earth. For weeks, you follow Coronado across mountains and deserts, hoping to find the Seven Cities. Your excitement grows in July when Zuñi Indians come to meet Coronado. You guess they are ambassadors from Cíbola.

"The king of Spain sends his greetings," Coronado says to welcome the ambassadors. Despite this friendly meeting, Coronado doesn't trust the Indians. The next morning, he orders the soldiers to put on their armor.

As you ride toward Cíbola, you keep your sword in your hand. Around a curve in the trail, you spot a tall building in the distance. "Cíbola!" you call. You kick your horse and he breaks into a gallop.

Turn the page.

Suddenly you stop. Instead of a city, you see a huge adobe building called a pueblo. Zuñi warriors standing in front gesture toward the pueblo and say "Háwikuh." You guess that this is their name for the pueblo. Meanwhile, Zuñi priests pour cornmeal in a line on the ground and make signs forbidding you to cross it.

Coronado unrolls a royal decree and reads it aloud. He doesn't care that it's not written in the Indians' language. "You must obey the King," he threatens, "or I'll punish you." Zuñi warriors and Spanish soldiers stare at each other across the cornmeal line.

"What are we waiting for?" you ask. "Come on!" You step over the cornmeal.

Coronado's soldiers attacked the Zuñi at Háwikuh.

Instantly, an arrow slices your throat. You fall to the ground, never to know if the golden cities of Cíbola exist or not.

THE END

To follow another path, turn to page 9.
To read the conclusion, turn to page 101.

The fleet reaches home in early November 1540. Coronado doesn't return until late 1542.

"Welcome home," you greet Coronado. "Captain Alarcón and I traveled up the Buena Guía River searching for you."

"I know. An officer found the buried letters," Coronado replies. "It's too bad we missed each other. The army needed supplies."

"But you found Cíbola. You're a rich man now," you assure him.

"No," Coronado shakes his head. "Cíbola is just an adobe pueblo. The Indians have no gold. Be thankful you sailed with Alarcón instead of chasing a fairy tale with me."

THE END

To follow another path, turn to page 9.
To read the conclusion, turn to page 101.

One December afternoon, you go riding with Coronado. "Want to race?" you ask.

"Of course," he grins. "Ready? Set. Go!" Suddenly, Coronado's saddle strap breaks. He falls from his horse. Before he can roll out of the way, one of your horse's hooves strikes him in the head. He survives the accident, although he is badly hurt. In the spring, he hasn't completely recovered.

"We wasted more than two years chasing fairy tales about golden cities," Coronado sighs. "It's time to go home." In April 1542, the army begins the long journey. Too weak to sit on a horse, Coronado rides in a litter hanging between two mules.

Turn the page.

Antonia de Mendoza served as the first viceroy of Mexico City.

Back in Mexico City, you and Coronado report to Viceroy Mendoza. "We didn't find the golden cities," you admit. "But we claimed new land for the king of Spain."

"That's true," Mendoza agrees. "Thanks to conquistadors like you, soon Spain will rule the entire New World."

THE END

To follow another path, turn to page 9.
To read the conclusion, turn to page 101.

It is a July day in 1540. You are sitting outside a large adobe building, called a pueblo, when a messenger arrives. He hurries inside to see your father, the chief. You quietly slip into the room. "A band of Spanish soldiers is coming here, to Háwikuh," the messenger reports. "The leader's name is Coronado."

"This is alarming news," your father says. He looks at you, standing in the doorway. "Go quickly. Bring everyone together for a meeting."

First you run to your mother, who is weaving on her loom. Nearby, you find your uncle repairing the irrigation ditches that carry water to the crops. Next you look for your brother. He's making adobe bricks. You search all over for your little sister. At last, you find her playing with the turkeys. You carry her to the pueblo.

Turn the page.

When you arrive, your father starts the meeting. "We don't know if the Spanish are friends or enemies," he says.

"Remember how Spanish conquistadors murdered the Aztec ruler and conquered his kingdom?" one man asks. "Now they want to conquer us Zuñi too."

"Coronado's soldiers are coming to capture slaves," another man warns.

"Maybe Coronado wants to make peace," a woman suggests.

"Chief," a priest says, "we all hope for peace. Send ambassadors to meet Coronado. But tell him not to enter our pueblo until after the summer ceremony." The people of Háwikuh agree to this plan and choose your brother and your uncle as ambassadors.

The Zuñi lived in several pueblos in present-day New Mexico.

❧ *To participate in the summer ceremony, turn to page* **64**.

❧ *To go with the ambassadors, turn to page* **65**.

The summer ceremony to celebrate the changing season begins the next morning. You gather with other members of your village and walk barefoot to the holy place where two rivers meet. Along the trail, a person dressed as the fire god sets fire to bushes to mark how far you have traveled. The smoke also symbolizes rain clouds.

In the evening, your brother brings you news. "One of the Spanish officers greeted us in a friendly way, but he won't turn back. By noon tomorrow, the soldiers will reach Háwikuh," your brother warns. "You should escape while you can."

➤ To escape, turn to page **68**.

➤ To return to Háwikuh, turn to page **70**.

The next day, you go with your brother and your uncle to meet Coronado. A few miles from Háwikuh, you point to a hill overlooking the Zuñi River. "From up there, we'll see the Spanish before they see us."

"Good idea," your uncle agrees, following you up the hill.

The Zuñi held ceremonies to celebrate their gods and important events.

Turn the page.

Soon you spot a group of soldiers on horseback. As they come closer, an officer sees you. He stops his horse and waves. You walk down to meet him.

The officer holds out his hand to greet you. He points to himself and says "Cárdenas."

"We have a message for Coronado," your uncle replies. "The Zuñi want peace. But Coronado cannot enter our pueblo during our summer ceremony. He must wait."

Cárdenas nods and smiles, although he clearly doesn't understand the Zuñi language. You make signs, trying to tell him to leave. He nods and smiles again. The meeting ends with an exchange of gifts. Your uncle returns to the pueblo to report that the Spanish seem friendly.

Coronado discovered that Háwikuh was a pueblo village instead of a grand city.

You and your brother stay to spy on the soldiers. After making a campfire, they polish their swords. "They're getting ready for a battle," you whisper. "Will they attack Háwikuh?"

"Maybe. I think Coronado is on his way to attack too," your brother replies. "By noon tomorrow, the Spanish will reach Háwikuh. You should escape while you can."

➤ To escape, turn to page **68**.

➤ To return to Háwikuh, turn to page **70**.

"Where should I go?" you ask your brother.

"Hide in the cave near the river. I'll come for you after the Spanish leave." As your brother hurries back to Háwikuh, you run toward the cave.

The cave is cold and damp. You want to start a fire, but you're afraid the soldiers will see it and discover you. Instead, you curl up in the back of the cave and wait for your brother to return.

You stay in the cave for one day and one night. On the second morning, you can't wait for your brother any longer. Avoiding the main trail, you slip toward Háwikuh. When you reach the fields, it's still too dark to see. But when the sun rises, you close your eyes to shut out the horrible scene.

Broken arrows and many dead bodies lie scattered on the ground. Two soldiers stand on the pueblo's roof, looking down triumphantly. The Spanish have conquered Háwikuh. You race away to warn other Indian villages that Coronado and his soldiers are coming.

THE END

To follow another path, turn to page 9.
To read the conclusion, turn to page 101.

When the Spanish arrive at Háwikuh, Zuñi warriors are guarding the pueblo. The priest pours a line of cornmeal on the ground and makes signs warning Coronado not to cross it.

Coronado makes a long speech. He doesn't speak the Zuñi language, but it is clear he's giving orders to your people. Then he stops. The warriors and the soldiers stare at each other across the line of cornmeal.

"What do the Spanish want?" you whisper to your brother. Before he can answer, one of the soldiers steps over the cornmeal line. Immediately, a Zuñi arrow hits the man in the throat. With a shout of command, Coronado draws his sword. The battle begins.

The Zuñi built adobe villages called pueblos.

Grabbing your spear, you run toward a bearded soldier. He swings his sword. It cuts deeply into your side. The intense pain causes you to collapse to the ground. As you take your last breath, you notice the sweet scent of cornmeal and dust.

THE END

To follow another path, turn to page 9.
To read the conclusion, turn to page 101.

René-Robert Cavelier, Sieur de La Salle, explored the Mississippi River Valley for France in 1682.

CHAPTER 4

Sieur de La Salle

It is December 1681. You live with your mother's people, the Miami Indians, in a village near the southern end of Lake Michigan. Your father is a hunter and trapper. His people, the French, have colonies around the Great Lakes.

One day your father returns to the village. "I have exciting news," he says. "Sieur de La Salle and his business partner, Henry de Tonti, are going to explore the Mississippi River. They're going to claim the heartland of America for France."

"Good. It's time the French take action," your mother replies. "Spain rules the southwest, and England is settling the east coast."

Turn the page.

Your father nods in agreement. "By building forts along the river, the French can keep the Spanish and the English from taking over the Mississippi Valley," he adds. "But the French will need Indian allies to succeed."

"I'm going with La Salle," you announce. "He always takes Indian guides. I know he'll need my skills on this expedition."

"You're also a good cook," your father says. "La Salle's men are gathering at Fort Miami on the St. Joseph River. You'd better hurry there."

"La Salle has probably crossed Lake Michigan by now," your mother says. "If I were you, I'd look for him near the western shore."

→ To head for Fort Miami, go to page 75.

→ To head toward Lake Michigan, turn to page 78.

When you arrive at Fort Miami, a Catholic priest welcomes you. "Good day, Father," you say. "I'm looking for La Salle. I want to volunteer for his expedition."

"I'm Father Zenobius Membré," the priest answers. "La Salle is hunting. Why don't you wait here for him?"

"Do priests go exploring?" you ask, sitting down by the fire.

"Absolutely," Father Membré explains. "Have you heard of Father Jacques Marquette?"

"No, I haven't," you reply. "But I would love to hear his story."

Turn the page.

Father Membré tells you the story of Marquette's famous journey. In 1673, Marquette set out with the French fur trader Louis Jolliet to find the mouth of the Mississippi River. "Marquette and Jolliet went far enough south to make certain the river flows into the Gulf of Mexico. Then they headed home," Father Membré continues. "La Salle plans to follow the river the whole way to the gulf and claim the surrounding land for France."

A hunter carrying a dead goose enters the fort. "La Salle," Father Membré says as he greets him, "this person wants to join our expedition."

"Can you paddle a canoe? Can you hunt and fish?" La Salle asks.

"Yes, I can do all those things," you answer. "I can cook too."

"Very good." La Salle shakes your hand. "You're hired. My business partner, Henry de Tonti, is waiting for us on the western shore of Lake Michigan. Tomorrow we'll meet him."

Turn to page **80**.

On the western shore of Lake Michigan, you meet a small group of Frenchmen. They're standing beside their canoes and staring at the frozen river.

"I guess we'll have to camp here until the ice melts," one of the men says.

"We can't wait until spring," the group's leader replies. He's a rugged-looking man who's missing his right hand.

"Excuse me," you approach him. "Why don't your men make sleds?"

"Good idea," he agrees. He orders the men to build sleds to carry the canoes and supplies. Then he turns to you. "I'm Henry de Tonti, La Salle's business partner. He and I plan to explore the Mississippi River. Do you want to come with us?"

You nod eagerly. "I would love to."

"You're hired," Tonti grins. "La Salle is at Fort Miami tonight. He'll cross Lake Michigan and join us here tomorrow morning. We'll start for the Mississippi as soon as he arrives."

Henry de Tonti came to North America with La Salle four years before the Mississippi River expedition in 1682.

Turn the page.

The next day, La Salle's group from Fort Miami meets Tonti and his men on the shore of Lake Michigan. Everyone pulls the sleds Tonti's men built to carry the canoes and supplies. You hike west from Lake Michigan to the frozen Illinois River. You drag your sled on the ice behind you.

"Open water," you call happily when you pass Lake Peoria and see that the Illinois River flows freely. Leaving your sled on the bank, you slide your canoe into the water for the swift ride to the Mississippi River.

In addition to 23 Frenchmen, a number of Indians, including women and children, joined La Salle's expedition.

In early February 1682, you dip your paddle into the mighty Mississippi. Day after day, the river carries the expedition south. The Missouri River roaring in from the west dumps muddy water into the Mississippi. The Ohio River pours in from the east, and the current under your canoe gets stronger. Along the banks of the Mississippi, you pass two deserted Indian villages. Every night for nearly three weeks, you camp on the shore. Each morning, you continue your voyage toward the Gulf of Mexico.

One afternoon in late February, the Frenchman Pierre Prudhomme invites you to go hunting with him.

➤ To stay in camp, turn to page 82.

➤ To go hunting with Prudhomme, turn to page 89.

"Where's Prudhomme?" you ask at breakfast the next morning. "I haven't seen him since he invited me to go hunting."

"Maybe he was kidnapped," Tonti suggests.

"We must find him," La Salle says. He orders some of the men to build a fort while the others look for Prudhomme. Four days pass. On the fifth day, you meet a group of Chickasaw Indians. When you question them about the missing Frenchman, they claim they haven't seen him. You keep searching.

On the 10th day, you see an animal clinging to a log floating down the river. "Look at that bear riding a log!" you laugh. As the log comes closer, you see that the animal is not a bear at all. It's Prudhomme!

You push a canoe into the water and paddle out to him. Prudhomme is very weak. You struggle to bring him to the shore.

"Did Indians kidnap you, Prudhomme?" Tonti wants to know.

"No," Prudhomme mumbles, "I got lost in the forest." He isn't hurt, but he's too weak to travel on with La Salle.

"We can't wait for you to recover. It's March already, and we must move on," La Salle tells Prudhomme. "You must stay at the new fort until we return. I've named it Fort Prudhomme, just for you."

➤ To continue the expedition with La Salle, turn to page **84**.

➤ To stay to take care of Prudhomme, turn to page **98**.

The men break camp, and the journey continues. For nearly a week, the Mississippi River carries the canoes south. On a foggy morning, near the mouth of the Arkansas River, you spot a village on the west bank. "Are the Acansa Indians in that village friendly?" you ask.

"I don't know," La Salle answers. "Let's cross to the other bank." When the fog disappears, a canoe full of Acansa warriors comes toward your group. Suddenly an arrow zips over Tonti's head.

"Don't shoot," La Salle warns. "They're testing our intentions. If we hold our fire, they will know we are peaceful." Everyone sits very still. The warriors paddle back to their village. Soon they return, bringing an invitation from their chief.

When you land at the village of Cappa, the chief holds a feast to honor La Salle. The food, songs, and dances remind you of celebrations in your mother's village. Cappa feels like home.

The Acansa Indians later became known as the Quapaw.

❧ To continue exploring with La Salle, turn to page **86**.

❧ To stay with the Acansa Indians, turn to page **92**.

After leaving Cappa, the Mississippi River pushes your canoe south for the next two weeks. You meet a few friendly Indians. But farther south, you pass many tribes who do not welcome La Salle. Every moment, you must be alert for danger from human enemies, wild animals, and sharp logs that can rip the canoes.

"We need more meat," you tell La Salle before breaking camp one morning.

"But we can't hunt here," he replies. "The land on both sides of the river is flooded."

"There are plenty of alligators. Let's catch one for dinner," you suggest. La Salle looks surprised, but he follows your advice. One of the men dangles a piece of fish on a line. A large alligator rises to snatch the bait. Quickly, you smash the alligator's skull with an axe. That night, you serve the Frenchmen alligator steaks.

By now, more than three months have passed since the expedition left Lake Michigan. One evening in early April 1682, you climb a tree to look around. You see acres of swampy land and, in the distance, blue water. That night, you're too excited to sleep.

In the morning, you paddle your canoe through the muddy river. First you feel a breeze. It tastes salty. Then you hear the sound of waves. "The ocean!" you call to La Salle. At last, you float into the Gulf of Mexico.

Later, La Salle holds a ceremony to claim the Mississippi Valley for France. He names it Louisiana, after King Louis XIV. La Salle puts the king's coat of arms on a large wooden cross. Meanwhile, the Frenchmen sing and shoot their muskets into the air.

Turn the page.

As you prepare for the return trip, Tonti takes you aside. "Now that the French officially own this land, we can build trading posts. Do you want to join La Salle and me in our fur trading business?" Tonti asks.

La Salle held a ceremony to claim the Mississippi River Valley for France in April 1682.

↠ To return to your mother's village, turn to page **94**.

↠ To join Tonti, turn to page **96**.

You swing your gun over your shoulder and go hunting with Prudhomme. In the mud near the river, you spot a large bear print. Using broken twigs and tufts of fur clinging to low branches as clues, you and Prudhomme track the bear. After two hours, you find a tree streaked with deep claw marks near an outcropping of rock. "We're close to the bear's den," you whisper.

A growl rumbles through the woods. As the bear comes out of its rocky den, Prudhomme shoots — and misses. Your shot hits the bear in the shoulder. The wounded bear charges. You and Prudhomme run, weaving around trees and splashing through streams. At last, the bear gives up the chase.

Turn the page.

"Let's go back to camp," you pant.

"Yes," Prudhomme agrees. "But where are we and how do we get back?"

In the darkening woods, you don't recognize any landmarks. You're lost. For 10 days, you and Prudhomme stumble through the forest searching for the camp.

"By now, La Salle has left without us. Let's try to catch up with him on the river," you tell Prudhomme. "We'll use this log as a canoe." You and Prudhomme push the log into the river and climb aboard.

Both of you cling to the log as it carries you swiftly downstream. You feel as if you've been riding forever, and you're almost too weak to hold onto the log. Suddenly, you hear voices along the riverbank.

La Salle didn't leave without you. His men spot you and Prudhomme floating on the river. They paddle out in their canoes and drag both of you to shore. The men carry you to the campsite. They have built a log fort there that La Salle names Fort Prudhomme.

But your time in the woods has left you feeling weak and sick. You are unable to continue the journey. You and Prudhomme must stay at the fort until La Salle and Tonti return to take you home.

THE END

To follow another path, turn to page 9.
To read the conclusion, turn to page 101.

"Come, you can live with my family," an Acansa named War-te-she says when La Salle, Tonti, and the others leave. You follow him across the village square, around the public meeting building, and past the pavilion used during ceremonies. War-te-she and his family live in a long rectangular house, built of poles and covered with bark. They share this house with several other families.

"Let's go fishing," War-te-she suggests after you put your belongings beside his family's fireplace. On the way to the river, he shows you the fields where the villagers raise corn, beans, pumpkins, and sunflowers. He leads you to a hollowed out cypress log floating near the riverbank. "This is my father's canoe," he explains. "Climb in."

The canoe rides so gently in the water that the fish don't notice it. Soon a huge fish swims beside you. Pointing to it, your friend hands you a small spear.

"Spear the fish?" you ask, moving your lips silently. War-te-she nods. Your hand trembles. You hold your breath and thrust the spear into the water.

"Good work," War-te-she says as you lift the glimmering fish from the water. You know you'll enjoy your new life with the Acansa Indians.

THE END

To follow another path, turn to page 9.
To read the conclusion, turn to page 101.

Tonti's offer is tempting, but you need to get back to your family. Now, instead of riding the Mississippi's current, you paddle your canoe upstream. In June, near Fort Prudhomme, La Salle becomes sick. "Go back to Canada without me," he orders Tonti. "Tell the governor we reached the Gulf of Mexico."

"I'll stay here with La Salle," you offer. Father Membré volunteers to stay too. With his help, you carry La Salle to the fort.

For six weeks, La Salle lies in bed, fighting death. You feed him soups made of healing herbs. Thanks to your care, he recovers. In late July, you and Father Membré pack the canoe. La Salle sits in the middle because he's still too weak to paddle. The three of you travel up the Mississippi River, up the Illinois River, and across Lake Michigan.

The Miami Indians lived in present-day Indiana, Illinois, and southern Michigan during the late 1600s.

"Thank you," La Salle says when you finally reach your village. "I must go to Canada, but I'll return soon. Will you help the French defend Louisiana?"

"I will," you reply. Then you wave goodbye and walk into your village to find your family.

THE END

To follow another path, turn to page 9.
To read the conclusion, turn to page 101.

You point your canoe north and paddle upstream, against the Mississippi River's current. In June 1682, La Salle suddenly becomes sick near Fort Prudhomme. "I'll stay here at the fort until I'm well. Father Membré will take care of me," he says. "You must help Tonti continue north."

"We plan to build forts like a row of stepping stones from the Great Lakes to the Gulf of Mexico," Tonti explains. "We already have Fort Miami near Lake Michigan. Next we need a fort on the Illinois River," he continues.

"You can count on me," you tell La Salle. Then, leaving him behind, you and Tonti lead the expedition up the Mississippi River. Later that summer, you enter the Illinois River.

"There's a great place for our fort," you exclaim one afternoon, pointing to a giant rock towering over the river. While the men make camp, you and Tonti climb the rock. "No enemies will dare to attack us up here," you say. "Yet traders can use the river as a highway for their canoes."

Tonti agrees. "I must return to Canada to get supplies. Meet me here in December, and we'll start building our fort. We'll name it Fort St. Louis."

THE END

To follow another path, turn to page 9.
To read the conclusion, turn to page 101.

You watch the canoes speed away down the river, then go back into the fort. "I'm sorry you had to stay," Prudhomme whispers from his bed. He's very weak. While he was lost, he had nothing to eat except wild berries. The best medicine for him is plenty of good food. You feed him hot stew and toasted corn bread. Thanks to your cooking, he recovers quickly.

Spring passes. One afternoon you hear a shout from the river. The expedition has returned. "Come quickly," Father Membré calls. "La Salle is very sick." You run to lift La Salle from a canoe and carry him into the fort. While Tonti leads the rest of the men back up the Mississippi, you and the priest stay at Fort Prudhomme with La Salle.

For six weeks, La Salle hangs between life and death. When he recovers at the end of July, you and Father Membré travel with him to Lake Michigan.

"Thank you," La Salle says when you reach your village. "I'm glad I could depend on you."

"You're welcome," you reply. "I'm glad I could care for you and Prudhomme." You shake hands with La Salle and return to your village to share your adventures with your family.

THE END

To follow another path, turn to page 9.
To read the conclusion, turn to page 101.

Contact with Spanish explorers introduced the Zuñi and other Indians to horses and guns.

CHAPTER 5

New Worlds

After 1492, Christopher Columbus made three more voyages. He always thought he'd reached the Indies. Other European explorers, however, realized he had discovered North and South America — the New World.

In 1494, the Treaty of Tordesillas gave a piece of South America to Portugal. Spain claimed the rest of the Americas. Spanish adventurers called conquistadors conquered American Indians, destroyed their civilizations and societies, and sent treasures back to Spain.

The conquistador Francisco Vázquez de Coronado believed rumors about golden cities. He led an expedition north from Mexico City in 1540.

After two years of searching, Coronado realized the rumors weren't true. He went home empty-handed. However, he paved the way for Spanish colonies in the area that later became the southwestern United States.

By the late 1500s, gold and silver from the Americas had made Spain a powerful nation. Other European nations became jealous. France and England sent explorers to North America in order to claim new land, set up trade networks, and start new colonies.

The French explorer and fur trader Sieur de La Salle traveled down the Mississippi River to the Gulf of Mexico in 1682. He named the Mississippi Valley "Louisiana" in honor of King Louis XIV. For the next 100 years, France fought Spain and England for control of this region.

In the end, none of these nations succeeded. The English colonists declared independence in 1776. They fought the American Revolution and created the United States.

In 1803, President Thomas Jefferson purchased the Louisiana Territory from France. Over time, the United States expanded even more. It claimed all the land from the Atlantic Ocean to the Pacific Ocean and from the Great Lakes to the Gulf of Mexico.

Columbus' voyage of 1492 marked the beginning of a new world for Indians as well as for Europeans. From the explorers, Indians learned about new tools. The southwestern Indians, for example, began using Spanish horses and guns.

Unfortunately, Europeans often treated Indians cruelly. Columbus and the colonists he brought to the Caribbean islands made the Tainos slaves. When the Zuñi wouldn't obey his orders, the Spanish conquistador Coronado attacked their pueblos.

Despite the attacks, the Indians never fully accepted Spanish rule. They fought for the freedom to follow their own way of life.

In other parts of North America, Indian tribes stood up for their rights when European and American settlers tried to claim land. They also took sides in the wars between European nations. Recognizing the value of friendship with the Indians, explorers such as La Salle often treated them as friends and trading partners.

Today, the United States is still a new world. It is a place where many cultures meet, bringing together different ways of life. It is a place to explore new foods, new languages, and new ideas.

TIME LINE

1492 — Christopher Columbus makes his first voyage to the New World.

1494 — Spain and Portugal sign the Treaty of Tordesillas. The treaty divides the New World between the two countries.

1502 — Columbus makes his fourth and last voyage to the New World.

1506 — Columbus dies in Valladolid, Spain.

1521 — Conquistador Hernán Cortés conquers the Aztec capital of Tenochtitlán. Mexico City is built on the ruins of the Aztec city. It becomes the capital of New Spain.

106

1532 — São Vicente, in present-day Brazil, becomes the first Portuguese settlement in the New World.

1540–1542 — Francisco Vázquez de Coronado explores the American Southwest in search of the Seven Cities of Cíbola. His search takes him as far north as present-day Kansas.

1554 — Coronado dies in Mexico City.

1598 — Mission San Gabriel becomes the first Spanish colony in present-day New Mexico.

1607 — English colonists establish Jamestown in present-day Virginia. It is the first successful English colony in the New World.

1608 — Samuel de Champlain founds Québec for France in present-day Canada.

1642 — The French create a settlement where Montreal is located in present-day Canada.

1673 — Jacques Marquette and Louis Jolliet explore the northern part of the Mississippi River.

1681–1682 — René-Robert Cavelier, Sieur de La Salle, explores the Mississippi River from Illinois to the Gulf of Mexico.

1687 — La Salle is murdered by his own men in present-day Texas.

1718 — The French found the city of New Orleans.

1803 — President Thomas Jefferson purchases the Louisiana Territory from France and doubles the size of the United States.

OTHER PATHS TO EXPLORE

In this book, you've seen how the events surrounding the exploration of the New World look different from five points of view.

Perspectives on history are as varied as the people who lived it. You can explore other paths on your own to learn more about what happened. Seeing history from many points of view is an important part of understanding it.

Here are some ideas for other New World points of view to explore:

+ When Columbus returned to the New World, he captured Tainos to help build new Spanish colonies. What was life like as a slave?

+ Coronado sent out small groups to explore areas away from his main trail. What was it like for the group that found the Grand Canyon?

+ Indian women and children joined La Salle's expedition down the Mississippi River. How do you think these Indians felt when they met the Acansa Indians?

READ MORE

Englar, Mary. *The Southwest Indians: Daily Life in the 1500s.* Mankato, Minn.: Capstone Press, 2006.

Kaufman, Mervyn D. *Christopher Columbus.* Mankato, Minn.: Capstone Press, 2004.

Mountjoy, Shane. *Francisco Coronado and the Seven Cities of Gold.* Philadelphia: Chelsea House, 2006.

Payment, Simone. *La Salle: Claiming the Mississippi River for France.* New York: Rosen, 2004.

INTERNET SITES

FactHound offers a safe, fun way to find Internet sites related to this book. All of the sites on FactHound have been researched by our staff.

Here's how:
1. Visit *www.facthound.com*
2. Choose your grade level.
3. Type in this book ID **1429613572** for age-appropriate sites. You may also browse subjects by clicking on letters, or by clicking on pictures and words.
4. Click on the **Fetch It** button.

FactHound will fetch the best sites for you!

GLOSSARY

adobe (uh-DOH-bee) — a brick building material made of clay mixed with straw and dried in the sun

conquistador (kon-KEYS-tuh-dor) — a leader in the Spanish conquest of North and South America during the 1500s

expedition (ek-spuh-DI-shuhn) — a long journey for a certain purpose, such as exploring

litter (LIT-ur) — a stretcher for carrying a sick or wounded person

missionary (MISH-uh-ner-ee) — a person sent by a church or religious group to teach that group's religion to others

musket (MUHSS-kit) — a gun with a long barrel that was used before the rifle was invented

Pope (POHP) — the head of the Roman Catholic Church

pueblo (PWEB-loh) — the Spanish word for village, usually consisting of stone and adobe buildings; also, an American Indian tribe of New Mexico and Arizona that lived in pueblos.

territory (TERR-uh-tor-ee) — an area under the control of a country